Party
in a Cup!

Easy Party Treats Kids Can Cook in Silicone Cups

By Julia Myall

Photographs by Greg Lowe

chronicle books · san francisco

*To my children and their friends—all my little
party animals—who inspired me.*

—J. M.

Text © 2010 by Julia Myall.
Photographs © 2010 by Greg Lowe.

Stitch Witchery is a registered trademark of
Prym Consumer USA Inc.

ISBN 978-0-8118-7188-4

Book design by Molly Baker.
Typeset in Neutra Text and Duality.

Manufactured by Toppan Excel, Guangzhou City,
Guangdong Province, China, in May 2010.

10 9 8 7 6 5 4 3 2 1

Kit materials conform to CPSIA 2008 safety standards.

Chronicle Books LLC
680 Second Street
San Francisco, California 94107
www.chroniclekids.com

Table of Contents

Introduction

Slumber Party A Night to Remember 10

Tea Party An Afternoon of Elegance 24

You're Invited!

Welcome to Your Party!

Party in a Cup! makes cooking for a party fun—and easy—from start to finish. All you need is in this kit: irresistible, colorful cups for the mouthwatering recipes you (and your friends!) will cook, step-by-step instructions for whipping those recipes up, party favor and decorating ideas, and more. You just need to bring your creativity and open mind, friends, and family to the table. Are you ready to party? Here we go!

Your Party Checklist

The secret ingredient to any great party is having a plan, staying organized, and getting a head start on preparation. Keep these party "musts" in mind and you'll guarantee yourself (and your friends) a great time.

Pick a theme. What type of party would you like to have? A slumber party? A tea party? Something to celebrate the end of the school year? Or maybe you'd like to get your girlfriends together for a day of pampering. The type of party you choose will help guide the rest of your choices, like the style of invitations, the decorations, and especially the food!

Think friends. Good company is key! You may be tempted to invite as many people as possible, but another party secret is that a perfect party isn't about quantity. The best way to guarantee a fun time for all is to invite friends who make you feel good, friends who get along well with each other, or people you'd just like to get to know better. A party is also a great way to have friends bond. Just remember: You can have as much fun with four friends as with fifteen!

Don't forget food! All the recipes you need for your party are in here! Use the six cups in this kit to cook up tasty treats that match your party's theme.

How will you have fun? You don't have to plan every part of your party to have a good time—you may just want to let the party take its course and be spontaneous! It can be good to have a general idea of how you want the party to play out, though. Think about games and things to do in the kitchen (or outdoors) to keep your guests entertained.

There's no wrong way to throw a party. You'll be bringing people together and giving them an experience they'll always remember. The recipes in this book will help you along the way, and hopefully they'll inspire you to see the kitchen as a key element of your party planning—and even the party experience itself!

Let's start cooking and get the party started!

Julia

Using Your Cups

You are now the proud owner of six colorful, bendable, party-ready silicone cups. Here are a few tips to keep in mind when you use them.

Wash 'em first

Wash and dry your cups before using them the first time.

Beware of hot stuff

Always use a hot pad or an oven mitt when handling cups that are fresh from the oven. Soon after cooking, the edges of the cup may be cool, but the part with the food in it will still be hot. So be careful! And don't forget about steam. All food releases steam when cooked, so watch out for hot steam when you're turning food out of your cups.

Stuck in the cup?

If something doesn't slide right out of a cup, give it more time to cool. Then try gently squeezing the base, using an oven mitt if the cup is still too warm to touch. Squeeze the base a few times in different spots, and then try to release the food again. If that doesn't help, slide a spoon or a butter knife between the edge of the cup and the food to help ease it out.

Clean up quickly!

Cleaning your cups is easy. You can give them a quick wash with a soapy sponge in the sink, or you can put them in the top rack of the dishwasher.

Kitchen Safety ⚠

You'll see this symbol ⚠ whenever a recipe step involves cutting with a sharp knife, using a kitchen appliance, or handling hot things. That's when you should be *especially* careful. Ask for adult help whenever the step requires it, or whenever you're doing something that's totally new to you.

Also, when an ingredient list calls for a pre-chopped item, ask an adult for help. No matter what, an adult should always be around when you're cooking so you can get help anytime you need it.

Slumber
Party

✦ ✦ Slumber Party ✦ ✦

A Night to Remember

Slumber parties are the classic party! You can have a spur-of-the-moment slumber party with just you and one or two friends. Or you can have a more planned party for a special occasion, like for your birthday or to celebrate the end of the school year with a handful of friends—or more. Here's what to keep in mind as you plan a slumber party your friends will never forget!

Slumber Party Basics

Who's sleeping over? Start with a guest list and invitations. Depending on the type of slumber party you're having, you can work that theme into your invitations. They can have a sleeping bag shape, or you can let your friends know they'll be heading over to your house for an overnight camping party with an invitation shaped like a tent. Be creative, and let your guests know you're really putting some thought into a fun night.

Serve it up! What makes a slumber party extra special is the food! You may want to use your cups and do some cooking before your guests arrive. Or you may want to make the kitchen a central part of your party! Bring everyone into the kitchen to make the party treats together.

Is anyone actually going to sleep? You may want to get your guests sleepy somehow, so try stepping out of the kitchen and getting crafty. You and your guests can make pretty pillowcases they can take home. And who says you can't spill secrets while you craft away?

Cheese Fondue

*Fondue is the ultimate party dip. Find out your friends' favorite cheeses.
Then serve 'em up in each cup.*

Ingredients for 6 cups:

¼ cup chopped broccoli

¼ cup bite-size pattypan squash pieces

¼ cup diced bread (like sourdough, rye, wheat, or French)

¼ cup cooked chopped potatoes

¼ cup pickle wedges

1½ cups grated cheese (your choice)

pattypan squash

To Prepare the Veggies and Bread

1. Place the broccoli and squash in a sauté pan with 1 inch of water. Bring to a boil. ⚠

2. Boil for 1 minute. Remove from the stove and drain the broccoli and squash in a colander. ⚠

3. Run cold water over the broccoli and squash to stop the cooking, and let drain.

4. Place the diced bread, veggies, and potatoes on a large platter.

To Make the Fondue

1. Place ¼ cup of the grated cheese in each cup.

2. Place the 6 cups of cheese in the microwave and heat for 20 seconds. Serve immediately with the bread and the veggies. ⚠

TRY IT THIS WAY!

Invite your guests to dip in! Place all the cheese cups in the middle of a large plate or platter. Arrange all the veggies and bread around the cups. Get some long forks or toothpicks and dive in. Here are some other items for dipping you may want to try: cooked pasta, sliced sausage, tortilla chips, apple and pear wedges, and pretzels.

Mini Pizza Pockets

Your guests won't be able to resist these mini pizza pockets in colorful cups! Take the party into the kitchen and have your guests toss the dough and then add their favorite toppings as fillings. Mama mini pizzas!

Ingredients for 6 mini pizza pockets:

1½ teaspoons active dry yeast
1 teaspoon honey
¾ cup warm water
2¼ cups all-purpose flour
1 teaspoon salt
1 tablespoon olive oil
1½ cups your choice of fillings (see page 15)

1. Preheat the oven to 400°F.

2. Place the yeast and the honey in the warm water and stir. Then wait about 2 minutes for bubbles to appear (this means the yeast is active).

3. Add the dry ingredients to a bowl.

4. After the bubbles appear in the yeast mixture add the olive oil, and then slowly pour it into the dry mixture. With adult help, use an electric mixer and mix on low speed until a ball of dough forms. ⚠

5. Place the dough on a floured surface and roll into a large circle with a rolling pin.

6. Use the cups like cookie cutters and press into the dough, making 12 disks.

7. Place one dough disk inside each cup. Use your fingers to press the dough firmly into the bottom.

8. Add your favorite fillings of choice to each cup, filling your cup three-fourths full.

9. Place a second dough disk on top to form the pizza pocket.

10. Place the cups on a baking sheet, put the sheet on the bottom rack of the oven, and bake for 20 minutes. Allow to cool and then serve. ⚠

TRY IT THIS WAY!

The filling ideas are endless, so have your guests top their own. Try marinara sauce, pesto, pepperoni, ham, pineapple, mozzarella string cheese, bell peppers (any color!), chicken, and olives.

Tostadas

These snacks are fiestas in a cup! Have a blast making these Tostadas with your party guests—and see how high you can stack your fillings!

Ingredients for 6 tostadas:

6 corn tortillas
6 tablespoons corn oil
½ pound ground beef
1 cup salsa
Pinch of salt
Pinch of pepper
One 8-ounce can beans, drained
1 cup chopped lettuce
½ cup grated Cheddar cheese
   (or, ¼ cup Cheddar and ¼ cup
   Monterey Jack)
¼ cup guacamole
¼ cup sour cream

1. Preheat the oven to 400°F.

2. Place three of the cups upside down on a baking sheet.

3. Using a pastry brush, coat both sides of the tortillas with the corn oil.

4. Drape an oiled tortilla over each cup.

5. Place a second cup over each tortilla to cover it.

6. Place the baking sheet in the oven and bake for 10 minutes. ⚠

7. Remove from the oven and remove the top cups using a fork. ⚠

8. Return the baking sheet to the oven and bake for 2 more minutes, or until the tortillas are golden brown. ⚠

9. Remove from the oven and let cool for 2 minutes. Repeat step 2 through 9 with the remaining tortillas.

10. Brown the beef in a sauté pan on the stove on medium heat. ⚠

11. Pour the beef into a colander to drain the excess liquid. ⚠

12. Pour the beef into a bowl and add ½ cup of the salsa and the salt and pepper. Mix together until well combined.

13. Time to fill your tostadas! Start with the beef on the bottom, and then add some beans, lettuce, cheese, guacamole, and salsa. Top with sour cream and serve.

Marshmallow Treats

Cereal isn't just for breakfast! These treats are crispy, crunchy, and the perfect sticky slumber party snack! (No milk required to enjoy!)

Ingredients for 6 marshmallow treats:

2 tablespoons butter
2 cups rice cereal
1½ cups marshmallows
Your choice of toppings (see page 19)

1. Place a small pat of butter in the bottom of each cup.

2. Place the cups in the microwave and heat for 10 seconds to melt the butter. ⚠

3. Mix together the rice cereal and the marshmallows in a bowl until well combined.

4. Fill each cup with the cereal and marshmallow mixture.

5. Top each cup with a small pat of butter.

6. Return the cups to the microwave and heat for 25 seconds. ⚠

7. Use the back of a spoon to press the mixture down.

8. Add your topping of choice and serve!

Add extra crunch and flavor to your crispy treats. Top your cups off with chocolate chips, white chocolate chunks, whipped cream and colored sprinkles, or even dried fruit.

Chocolate Mousse

Your guests won't be able to resist this mouthwatering chocolate delight. It's rich, creamy, and oh-so-simple (and fun) to make!

Ingredients for 6 cups:

½ cup chocolate chips
1 cup heavy whipping cream
1 teaspoon vanilla
Your choice of toppings (see page 21)

1. Melt the chocolate chips in a microwave-safe bowl in the microwave for 15 seconds. Take out, stir, and if not melted, return to the microwave for an additional 10 seconds. Be careful not to burn the chocolate.

2. With adult help, whip the heavy whipping cream with an electric mixer until medium peaks form. Then stir in the vanilla.

3. Set aside three tablespoons of the whipped cream.

4. Pour the melted chocolate into the rest of the whipped cream and mix with a spatula until combined.

5. Spoon some of the chocolate mousse in each cup. Then place a dollop of whipped cream on top.

6. Refrigerate the cups for 2 hours. Add your favorite toppings before serving.

TRY IT THIS WAY!

Toppings give this mousse extra pizzazz! Add mini chocolate chips, colored sprinkles, white chocolate shavings or spears, chopped cookies, fresh berries, or bananas.

21

Pretty Pillowcases

You may not sleep at your slumber party, but send your guests home with these pretty pillowcases to remember the night by!

Materials for 6 pillowcases:

Fabric pens or paints
1 yard colorful fabric
Scissors
1 package Stitch Witchery
6 standard-size pillowcases
Iron
2 yards colorful satin ribbon

1. With a fabric pen, trace a cup upside down 6 times on the fabric.

2. Cut out the traced shapes.

3. Place Stitch Witchery on the underside of each cutout shape.

4. Place the cutouts on a pillowcase and then iron on according to the Stitch Witchery directions. ⚠

5. Use fabric pens or paint to decorate the pillowcase as desired.

6. Cut the ribbon into 6 pieces and use a piece to tie each pillowcase closed. Send each guest home with a pillowcase packed with goodies, like hair accessories, mini flashlights, journals—your friends' favorite things. ⚠

Tea Party

An Afternoon of Elegance

Tea parties are some of the most gorgeous parties. The table is set beautifully, your guests are dressed up, and the food is delicate, delicious, and a sight to behold! Here's how to create an unforgettable tea party for you and your friends.

Tea Party Basics

Make your invitations special. Add a special touch to your tea party right from the start! Make invitations out of beautiful lace paper, or cut your invitations in the shape of a teapot or the shape of a tea bag. Use a calligraphy pen or colored pens to write out when and where the party will occur.

Get dressed up! Ask your guests to dress up for your party. Write, "Wear your favorite party dress!" or "Wear your prettiest blouse with jeans" on the invitation. You can also ask your guests to bring a stuffed animal or doll to sit with them at the table.

Set the table sweetly. Pick beautiful flowers and place them in little vases so that you can still see your guests across the table. Mix and match beautiful cups and set your favorite teapot—or tea*pots*—on your table.

Tiny treats. Tea party food is usually presented in bite-size servings. Remember, tea parties are all about sharing special moments with your guests, and passing food really gets people talking!

Time for tea. You can also serve your guests freshly made lemonade, hot chocolate, juice, or fruit punch. Be sure to have sugar and milk on the table for your guests to add to their tea.

Scones

Scones are a staple of any English tea party. These buttery bites are fantastic when served with the Strawberry Butter (page 28), any sweet butter, or even a savory piece of ham.

Ingredients for 6 scones:

1¾ **cups all-purpose flour**
½ **teaspoon salt**
½ **tablespoon baking powder**
1 **tablespoon sugar**
3 **tablespoons butter**
1 **egg**
⅓ **cup heavy cream**

1. Preheat the oven to 450°F.

2. Combine the flour, salt, baking powder, and sugar in a medium mixing bowl.

3. Add the butter to the dry mixture, 1 tablespoon at a time, and mix with a fork until pea-size crumbs form.

4. Add the egg and the cream. Stir the mixture with a spoon until smooth.

5. Spoon the mixture into the cups, filling them up halfway.

6. Place the cups on a baking sheet and bake for 7 to 9 minutes. ⚠

7. Let the scones cool for 5 minutes and then turn them out of the cups.

Depending on what type of tea you're serving, you may want sweet or savory scones. Try adding one or more of these options to the recipe.

- ½ cup shredded Cheddar cheese and ¼ cup diced scallions
- ¼ cup diced ham and ½ cup cheese of choice
- ½ cup dried fruit (raisins, currants, or chopped apricots)
- 1 tablespoon grated citrus zest (lemon or orange)
- ½ cup pecans, chopped into small pieces
- ½ cup walnuts, chopped into small pieces
- ¼ cup candied ginger

Keep these extras on hand for guests to spread on their scones: lemon curd, jelly, jam, Nutella, cream cheese, compote. Serve in pretty, small bowls, and include a small serving spoon or knife near each for easy spreading.

Strawberry Butter

You'll want to spread this sweet-flavored butter on just about everything! Try it with the Scones (page 26), and don't be surprised when your guests ask for more!

Ingredients for 6 cups:

1 pint strawberries, washed and tops removed

1 pound (4 sticks) butter, at room temperature

1. Pat the strawberries dry.

2. With adult help, use a blender or electric mixer to cream together the butter and all but three of the strawberries until smooth. ⚠

3. Use a spatula to scrape the butter mixture out of the blender and generously fill each cup.

4. Place the cups in the refrigerator for 1 hour, or until the mixture hardens.

5. Slice the reserved strawberries and arrange a few slices in each cup. Place a cup near each of your guests at the table.

Cucumber Canapés

These open-faced sandwiches are tea party classics. Canapés— decorative, bite-size delights—are fun to make and even more fun to pop into your mouth.

Ingredients for 12 canapés:

1 loaf of bread (your choice), sliced
6 tablespoons cream cheese
¼ teaspoon grated lemon zest
¼ teaspoon chopped fresh dill
1 cucumber, thinly sliced

1. Place the bread slices on a cutting board.

2. Take a cup and turn it upside down, pressing it into the bread like a cookie cutter. You may need to trace the cup with a butter knife, with adult help. Repeat to make 12 disks total. ⚠

3. Place the cream cheese in a bowl.

4. Add the lemon zest and the dill to the cream cheese and blend together with a spatula.

5. Spread the cream cheese on each bread disk.

6. Place a few cucumber slices on top of each disk.

7. Turn each cup over and place an open-faced sandwich on each one.

Chicken Salad Sandwiches

Here's a classic tea party sandwich for your party. Use any type of bread, or mix and match breads for a checkerboard look!

Ingredients for 6 sandwiches:

2 cups chopped cooked chicken breast
2 tablespoons mayonnaise
1 stalk celery, chopped into small pieces
¼ teaspoon Dijon mustard
1 teaspoon chopped fresh parsley, plus 6 sprigs for garnish
1 loaf of pumpernickel bread (or bread of your choice)

1. Place the chicken, mayonnaise, celery, Dijon mustard, and chopped parsley in a bowl and mix well.

2. Place the bread on a cutting board. Take a cup and turn it upside down, pressing it on top of the bread like a cookie cutter. Repeat 11 times.

3. Spoon a teaspoon of the chicken mixture onto each bread disk.

4. Add a bread disk to top off your sandwich, garnish with a sprig of parsley, and serve in the cups.

Cinnamon Yorkshire Pudding

Yorkshire pudding isn't just for the holidays—it's also the perfect addition to a tea party table. Serve these wonderful puffed-up treats warm with the Strawberry Butter (page 28). They'll steal the show!

Ingredients for 6 puddings:

2 eggs
¾ cup milk
¾ cup all-purpose flour
Pinch of cinnamon
⅛ teaspoon sugar
2 tablespoons butter

1. Preheat the oven to 425°F.

2. Beat the eggs with an electric mixer until they look pale yellow in color. ⚠

3. Add the milk, flour, cinnamon, and sugar, and whisk the ingredients together until smooth.

4. Cut the butter into 6 pieces and place 1 piece in each cup. ⚠

5. Microwave the butter in the cups for 10 seconds, or until melted. ⚠

6. Remove from the microwave and pour the melted butter into the batter. Stir the mixture with a spoon until smooth.

7. Pour the batter into the buttered cups, filling each one half full.

8. Place the cups on a baking sheet and bake for 15 minutes, or until a fork comes out clean. ⚠

Éclairs

Éclairs were one of my favorite desserts when I was a kid. An éclair can be filled with anything—pastry cream, whipped cream, and even fresh fruit. My favorite filling is ice cream!

Ingredients for 6 éclairs:

Éclairs
2 eggs
½ cup water
4 tablespoons butter
½ cup all-purpose flour
1 tablespoon sugar
Pinch of salt

Chocolate Glaze
½ cup chocolate chips
½ cup heavy whipping cream
1 tablespoon butter

Filling
2 cups whipped cream

To Make the Éclairs

1. Preheat the oven to 375°F.

2. In a bowl, beat the eggs with an electric mixer until they look pale yellow in color. Set aside.

3. Place the water and butter in a saucepan and bring to a boil. Then turn off the heat. ⚠

4. Sift the dry ingredients together in a bowl.

5. Add the dry ingredients to the water and butter. ⚠

6. Stir the mixture together until it looks like a ball of dough.

(Recipe continued on next page.)

7. Place the dough ball in a bowl. With adult help, use an electric mixer to mix on low for five minutes, or until the mixture has cooled to room temperature. ⚠

8. Add the eggs to the ball of dough.

9. Continue to mix on low until the dough is sticky. ⚠

10. Scoop the mixture into the cups, filling each one three-quarters full.

11. Place the cups on a baking sheet and bake for 30 minutes. Then turn off the oven and let the cups remain there for 15 more minutes. ⚠

12. Remove from the oven and let cool for 10 minutes. ⚠

13. With adult help, cut the tops off of each éclair. Set the tops aside on a plate. ⚠

To Make the Glaze

1. Place the chocolate glaze ingredients in a microwave-safe bowl and microwave on high for 1 minute, or until melted. ⚠

2. Remove from the microwave and whisk the mixture until smooth.

To Assemble the Éclairs

1. Top each éclair bottom with 2 tablespoons of the filling.

2. Place the tops back on each éclair bottom.

3. Pour the glaze over each éclair.

4. Arrange the éclairs on a large platter and serve.

Angel Food Cake

These sweet cakes are like little fluffy clouds that will delight everyone at your table. Add a fresh berry to each one for a burst of color!

Ingredients for 6 cakes:

10 egg whites
¼ teaspoon salt
1 teaspoon cream of tartar
1¾ cups sugar
1 teaspoon vanilla
1¼ cups cake flour

1. Preheat the oven to 325°F.

2. With adult help, beat the egg whites with an electric mixer until foamy bubbles form. ⚠

3. Add the salt and the cream of tartar and continue beating the mixture until soft peaks form. ⚠

4. Add the sugar and vanilla and continue beating the mixture until stiff peaks form. ⚠

5. Using a spatula, fold the flour into the egg whites until well blended.

6. Spoon the batter into the cups, filling each one two-thirds full.

7. Place the cups on a baking sheet and bake for 20 minutes, or until a toothpick comes out clean. ⚠

8. Remove from the oven and allow to cool for 10 minutes. ⚠

Boston Tea Cakes

These are the perfect cakes for dipping in your tea or hot chocolate—and they're actually made with tea! Peach-flavored black tea is used in this recipe, but you can infuse your cakes with any tea. Choose your favorite!

Ingredients for 6 cakes:

Cakes

¾ cup milk
1 peach-flavored black tea bag
    (or tea of choice)
½ cup (1 stick) butter, at room
    temperature
1 cup sugar
3 eggs
1½ cups all-purpose flour
½ teaspoon baking powder
¼ teaspoon baking soda
Pinch of salt

(Ingredients continued on next page.)

To Make the Cakes

1. Preheat the oven to 350°F.

2. In a pot over medium heat, bring the milk to a boil, then add the tea bag. ⚠

3. Remove the pot from the heat and steep the tea bag for 5 minutes. ⚠

4. With adult help, mix together the butter and the sugar in an electric mixer. ⚠

5. Add the eggs to the butter and sugar mixture and continue to mix until well blended. ⚠

(Recipe continued on next page.)

Ingredients continued:

Glaze

¼ cup chocolate chips
¼ cup heavy whipping cream,
    plus more as needed
1 tablespoon butter

Cream Filling

½ cup condensed milk
½ cup heavy whipping cream
¼ teaspoon vanilla

6. Add all the dry ingredients and continue mixing until well combined. ⚠

7. Pour in the milk and tea mixture. Stir with a spoon until the mixture is smooth and well combined.

8. Spoon the mixture into the 6 cups, filling each one two-thirds full.

9. Place the cups on a baking sheet and bake for 15 minutes, or until a fork comes out clean. Allow to cool for 10 minutes. ⚠

To Make the Glaze

1. Place the chocolate chips and heavy whipping cream in a microwave-safe bowl and microwave for 20 seconds, or until the ingredients have melted. Whisk together the chocolate and whipping cream until smooth enough to pour. ⚠

2. Add the butter. Stir until smooth. (If too thick, add an additional ¼ teaspoon at a time of the heavy whipping cream until smooth enough to pour.) ⚠

To Assemble the Cakes

1. With adult help, mix the cream filling ingredients together with an electric mixer until smooth.

2. Carefully cut the cooled cakes in half horizontally and set the top parts aside on a plate.

3. Fill the cake in the cup with a dollop of cream. Then place the cups in the refrigerator and allow to cool for ½ hour. Make the glaze while the cakes are cooling.

4. Put the tops of the cakes back on each filled cup.

5. Pour the chocolate glaze on top of each cake.

Lavender Pouches

Craft these sweet-smelling keepsake pouches at your party. They're the perfect party favors!

Materials for 6 pouches:

½ yard fabric of your choice
Scissors
1 cup fresh lavender
1 yard satin ribbon

1. Cut the fabric into 6 equally-sized squares.

2. Put a square of fabric in each cup and fill with 2 tablespoons of fresh lavender.

3. Cut the ribbon into 6 pieces. Gather the fabric at the top of each cup and tie with a ribbon.

Summer
Party

Summer Party

Fun in the Sun

When it's warm outside and the sky is blue, it's the perfect time to have a party. The key is to make the most of the great outdoors, giving you and your guests a time to remember in nature. You can throw a party in the park, at a pool, in your backyard, or even on a porch or terrace. Use fruits and veggies that are in season as you celebrate the summer!

Summer Party Basics

Theme it! Make the most of your summer theme by asking your guests to come dressed for fun in the sun. Do you want everyone to wear bathing suits? Their favorite summer dress? Shorts and tees? If so, include that info in your invitation. You'll also want to let your guests know if there will be water games or sprinklers. If so, they should bring a towel or even an extra change of clothes.

Cool down. You'll want to keep your guests cool in the heat, especially if your party is in the middle of summer. Be sure to have a lot of ice on hand—you can even color your ice by adding 2 drops of food coloring to each cube before freezing.

Fun in the sun. You don't need a pool to have a blast at your summer party. Play tag with water balloons, or assign teams and send your guests on a scavenger hunt. If you do have a pool, have a belly-flop contest, or suggest that you and your guests choreograph dances to your favorite tunes—then perform them for each other.

Summer Dips

Dips are a summer party staple. These three taste great with veggies, any type of chips, and pitas. Serve one or all three at your party, and your guests will be sure to dip in and thank you!

Ingredients for 6 cups:

Hummus Dip

**1 roasted red pepper, seeded
   and sliced**
1 garlic clove
Pinch of salt
Pinch of pepper
**One 16-ounce can garbanzo
   beans (chickpeas), drained**
**2 tablespoons lemon
   juice**

To Make the Hummus Dip

1. With adult help, place all the ingredients in a food processor and mix for about 2 minutes, or until smooth. ⚠

2. Fill each cup with the dip.

3. If you wish, garnish each cup with a slice of red pepper or top each cup off with a whole garbanzo bean.

Hot Crab Dip

½ pound cooked crab meat
2 tablespoons mayonnaise
½ teaspoon Dijon mustard
¼ teaspoon Worcestershire sauce
Pinch of garlic salt
½ teaspoon chopped flat-leaf
   parsley
1 green onion, roughly chopped
¼ teaspoon grated lemon zest
¼ cup bread crumbs

Yogurt Dip

1½ cups plain or Greek yogurt
1 garlic clove (or ⅛ teaspoon
   garlic powder)
⅛ cup walnuts
1 teaspoon chopped chives
1 tablespoon chopped fresh dill

To Make the Hot Crab Dip

1. Preheat the oven to 350°F.

2. With adult help, place all the ingredients except the bread crumbs in a food processor and blend on the pulse setting for 1 minute to chop the ingredients. ⚠

3. Fill each cup with the dip and sprinkle the bread crumbs on top.

4. Place the cups on a baking sheet and bake for 15 minutes. ⚠

5. Allow to cool for 5 minutes and then serve warm. ⚠

To Make the Yogurt Dip

1. With adult help, place all of the ingredients in a food processor and mix for 2 minutes, or until smooth. ⚠

2. Fill each cup with the dip and garnish with a dill sprig or a walnut.

Shrimp Cuptails

*Add an ocean element to your summer party scene with shrimp!
This is a great way to serve up a classic in your colorful cups.*

Ingredients for 6 cuptails:

12 ounces shrimp cocktail sauce
42 pieces of cooked shrimp,
   with tails on
1 lemon

1. Fill each cup half full with the cocktail sauce.

2. Place 7 shrimp around the inside of each cup with the tails pointing out.

3. With adult help, slice the lemon into 6 wedges.

4. Put 1 wedge in the center of each cup.

5. To keep your cuptails cool when serving, put ice in a bowl and place the cups on top of the ice.

Caesar Salad with Parmesan Baskets

This salad in an edible basket is a feast for the eyes! Be polite and dive in with a fork and knife, or just pick 'em up and take a big crunchy bite!

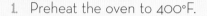

Ingredients for 6 baskets:

2 cups shredded Parmesan cheese
1 head of romaine lettuce, washed
   and cut into bite-size pieces
4 tablespoons Caesar salad
   dressing of choice
1 cup croutons
Pinch of salt
Pinch of pepper

1. Preheat the oven to 400°F.

2. Place the cups upside down on a baking sheet.

3. Sprinkle all but 2 tablespoons of the cheese over the top and around the sides of the cups.

4. Bake for 5 minutes, or until the cheese is golden brown. Remove from the oven and let cool for 10 minutes. ⚠

5. With a spatula, gently remove the cups from the pan. Turn over onto a plate and pull out the cups from the Parmesan baskets with your fingers. Leave the baskets on the plate.

6. Toss the lettuce, the remaining Parmesan cheese, dressing, croutons, salt, and pepper in a bowl until well mixed.

7. Place a heaping spoonful of the salad inside each Parmesan basket and serve.

Sliders

These mini burgers are the perfect little bites for a pool party. You can make them ahead of time or grill them right there by the pool. Having your guests' favorite toppings on hand will stir up smiles all around!

Ingredients for 6 sliders:

Buns

½ teaspoon active dry yeast
¼ teaspoon honey
¾ cup warm water
1¾ cups all-purpose flour
¼ teaspoon salt
1 tablespoon olive oil

Patties

1 pound ground beef
Pinch of garlic salt
6 ounces Cheddar
   cheese, shredded

To Make the Buns

1. Place the yeast and the honey in the warm water and stir. Then wait about 2 minutes for bubbles to appear.

2. Add the dry ingredients to a bowl.

3. After the bubbles appear in the yeast mixture add the olive oil, and then slowly pour it into the dry mixture.

4. With adult help, use an electric mixer and mix on low speed until a ball of dough forms. ⚠

5. Transfer the dough to a floured countertop or cutting board and knead it for 3 minutes.

6. Place in a lightly oiled bowl and cover it with a damp towel. Let the dough rise for 1 hour.

7. Turn the dough out onto a floured cutting board,

and pound it down with your fist. Then roll the dough into a long cylinder.

8. With adult help, use a butter knife to cut the dough into six 1-inch-thick disks. Place a disk in each cup. ⚠

9. Let the dough rise for 1 hour in the cups.

10. Preheat the oven to 400°F.

11. Place the cups on a baking sheet and bake for 20 minutes. Allow to cool before turning the buns out and cutting them in half horizontally. ⚠

To Make the Patties

1. Preheat the oven to 350°F.

2. Mix together the ground beef and the garlic salt.

3. Place 2 tablespoons of the ground beef in each cup.

4. Spoon 1 tablespoon of the cheese on top of the beef. Add more beef on top of the cheese.

5. Place the cups on a baking sheet and bake for 25 minutes. ⚠

6. Place the patties between the buns. Don't forget to add your favorite condiments!

TRY IT THIS WAY!

Here are some topping ideas: pineapple, barbecue sauce, mushrooms, avocados, red onion slices, tomatoes, relish and pickles (sweet and sour), and capers.

Pineapple Upside-Down Cupcakes

Good party hosts like to plan ahead, so you can make this a day or two ahead and it will still taste fantastic! Serve these cupcakes warm with vanilla ice cream or with whipped cream. No matter how you serve 'em, your guests are in for a tropical treat!

Ingredients for 6 cupcakes:

1¼ cups (2½ sticks) plus
   4 tablespoons butter, at room
   temperature
1 cup granulated sugar
1 tablespoon white balsamic vinegar
3 teaspoons vanilla
3 eggs
2 cups all-purpose flour
2 teaspoons baking powder
⅛ teaspoon salt
⅓ cup heavy whipping cream
6 tablespoons brown sugar
One 8-ounce can unsweetened
   pineapple chunks, drained

1. Preheat the oven to 350°F.

2. With adult help, cream together 1¼ cups of the butter and the granulated sugar with an electric mixer on medium speed. ⚠

3. Add the vinegar, vanilla, and eggs to the mixer bowl and beat on low for 1 minute, or until the ingredients are blended. ⚠

4. Sift together the flour, baking powder, and salt.

5. Add the dry ingredients to the wet ingredients and blend until smooth. ⚠

6. Add the whipping cream to the mixture and stir with a spoon until well combined.

7. With adult help, cut the remaining 4 tablespoons butter into 6 even cubes with a butter knife, and place 1 cube in each cup. ⚠

8. Add 1 tablespoon of brown sugar to each cup.

9. Add a spoonful of pineapple chunks to each cup.

10. Microwave the cups for 15 seconds, or until the butter has melted. ⚠

11. Add a spoonful of batter to each cup.

12. Place the cups on a baking sheet and bake for 20 minutes, or until a fork comes out clean. ⚠

13. Let cool in the cups for 10 minutes. Then carefully turn each cup over onto a large plate to release the cupcakes.

TRY IT THIS WAY!

If you choose to bake these a day or two before your party, let the cupcakes cool for an hour. Then remove them from the cups, place on a plate, and cover tightly with plastic wrap. Refrigerate until you are ready to serve.

Macaroons

These chewy tropical treats are infused with summer! Dip these delights in chocolate, add sprinkles to the top, or just eat them plain. Don't be surprised when your guests ask for more!

Ingredients for 6 macaroons:

¾ **cup almond meal**
¾ **cup powdered sugar**
1 **cup egg whites (6 eggs)**
2 **tablespoons granulated sugar**
½ **cup coconut flakes**

1. Preheat the oven to 400°F.

2. Combine the almond meal and the powdered sugar in a bowl.

3. Add ½ cup of the egg whites to the bowl and mix with a spoon until blended.

4. In another bowl, whisk the remaining egg whites with the granulated sugar until soft peaks form.

5. Add the coconut to the almond meal mixture.

6. With a spatula, fold the whisked whites into the almond meal mixture.

7. Spoon the mixture into the cups, filling them two-thirds full.

8. Place the cups on a baking sheet and bake for 15 minutes. Then cool and serve. ⚠

Spa
Party

Spa Party

An Afternoon of Pampering

Sometimes you just want to pamper yourself and your friends! A spa party captures the spirit of a spa, which is where people go to relax and do what's good for their mind and body. Spa parties are easy parties to throw because you just need lots of good things to read, plenty of refreshing drinks, and healthful, tasty treats to munch on! Oh, and bring on the nail polish! A great spa party activity is to paint your fingernails and toenails with your friends. Yes, you're going to send your guests home with pretty feet!

Spa Party Basics

Bring your own . . . When you invite your guests, ask them to bring their own brush, beauty products, and even their favorite nail polish. If you have lots of different nail polish colors on hand, you can make pretty hearts and flowers on your nails. The more options the more fun!

The setting is everything. Since spas are all about getting pampered, you'll want your guests to feel like your party is where they'll totally relax! Arrange a room with lots of pillows and have pitchers of water filled with fresh berries, peaches, and even cucumbers. Be sure to ask your friends to bring their own towels and robes for the best spa experience ever.

Pick your products. For your main activity (when you're not eating) you'll want your guests to feel pampered. Whether it is facial products, nail products, or hair products, pick your favorites, or spread out a selection for your friends to choose from.

Party with fresh food. The treats you serve should all have a healthy, refreshing element. Think fresh fruits and veggies, and don't forget the mint! When your friends leave your party, they'll feel energized and ready to do anything after all that pampering!

Cold Cucumber Soup

Cucumbers are calm and cool—spa staples! This soup will refresh you and your guests and capture the true "spa" experience.

Ingredients for 6 cups:

½ yellow onion, diced
2 tablespoons butter
2 cups chicken stock
⅛ teaspoon dill seed
1 cucumber, cut in half lengthwise
   and seeded
½ cup heavy whipping cream or
   plain yogurt
Chopped fresh dill, for garnish

1. Sauté the onion in the butter in a frying pan on medium heat until transparent. ⚠

2. Turn off the heat and add the chicken stock and dill seed to the onions. Let cool for 5 minutes. ⚠

3. Once cooled, add the onion mixture to a blender and, with adult help, purée on medium speed with the cucumber. ⚠

4. Cover the onion mixture with plastic wrap and refrigerate for a half hour.

5. Remove the mixture from the refrigerator, add the cream or yogurt, return to the blender, and blend until well combined. ⚠

6. Pour the soup into the cups and garnish with dill.

Gazpacho

This medley is packed with veggies and lots of the vitamins you and your guests need to feel energized.

Ingredients for 6 cups:

3 tomatoes (2 diced, 1 cut into
   6 slices)
½ cucumber, cut in half lengthwise
   and seeded
½ yellow bell pepper, seeded and
   chopped into small pieces
1 small garlic clove, minced
1 teaspoon olive oil
½ teaspoon red wine vinegar
Pinch of salt
Pinch of pepper
1 cup water or tomato juice
⅛ cup croutons

1. With adult help, purée all the ingredients (except the tomato slices and the croutons) in a blender, adding the water or tomato juice last. ⚠

2. Pour the gazpacho into a large bowl, and then ladle into the cups.

3. Top off each cup with croutons and a slice of tomato.

Sushi Stacks

This Japanese-style treat is so much fun to make. Stack up sushi rice, avocado, and seaweed; then put anything you like in between!

Ingredients for 6 stacks:

1⅛ cups water
1 cup short-grain rice or sushi rice
2 teaspoons sugar
2 tablespoons rice vinegar
½ teaspoon salt
4 sheets of seaweed
1 avocado, sliced
¼ pound crab meat
Soy sauce

1. With adult help, pour the water into a pot and bring to a boil. ⚠

2. Add the rice to the water. Reduce the heat to low and simmer, uncovered, for 10 minutes. ⚠

3. Turn the heat off and cover the pot for an additional 10 minutes to let the rice soak up the water. ⚠

4. Place the sugar, rice vinegar, and salt in one of the cups and microwave for 10 seconds, or until the sugar is dissolved. ⚠

5. With adult help, pour the cooked rice onto a baking pan lined with plastic wrap. ⚠

6. Drizzle the vinegar-sugar mixture over the rice while turning the rice with a fork.

7. With a butter knife or scissors, trace or cut 6 small disks onto the seaweed using the bottom

side of a cup. Repeat 6 more times. You now have 12 small disks. ⚠

8. Repeat step 7 using the top side of the cup to make 6 large disks.

9. Place plastic wrap in the center of the cups, with extra plastic rolled over the edges.

10. Place 2 small seaweed disks in each cup.

11. Layer your stacks, starting with the rice.

12. Place an avocado slice on top of the rice and pat down with your fingers.

13. Place 1 teaspoon of the crab on top of the avocado.

14. Finally, place more of the rice on top of the crab, and then top it off with a large seaweed disk.

15. Remove each sushi stack by placing a plate on top of each cup. Then, turn the plate over along with your stack. Take off your cup and remove the plastic.

16. Place back in the cups if you wish, and serve with soy sauce.

TRY IT THIS WAY!

Add crunch and personality to your sushi stacks. Try tomato slices, cucumber slices, jicama, bean sprouts, alfalfa sprouts, and even carrot slices.

Couscous and Chicken with Mint Pesto

Couscous is a grain that's good for you and tasty! Chicken packs a protein punch, and the mint makes this ultra-refreshing!

Ingredients for 6 cups:

6 sprigs of mint
1 garlic clove
4 tablespoons olive oil
1 teaspoon lemon juice
2 tablespoons pine nuts
Pinch of salt
Pinch of pepper
6 chicken breasts, uncooked
  and cut into strips
1½ cups chicken stock
1½ cups couscous

1. Preheat the oven to 350°F.

2. With adult help, make the mint pesto in a blender by puréeing the mint, garlic, olive oil, lemon juice, pine nuts, salt, and pepper on low speed. (Save 6 mint leaves for step 11.) ⚠

3. With a plastic spoon, scoop out the mint pesto and place in a freezer bag.

4. Add the chicken to the bag and be sure it's covered with the mint pesto. Let marinate in the refrigerator for 1 hour.

5. Remove the chicken from the bag and discard the remaining mint pesto. Place the chicken in a large baking dish. Bake for 25 minutes. Remove from the oven and allow to cool. ⚠

6. Place the 6 cups on a microwave-safe plate that fits in your microwave. ⚠

7. Pour ¼ cup chicken stock into each cup.

8. Microwave on high for 1 minute and 30 seconds, or until you see bubbles at the bottom of each cup.

9. With adult help, remove from the microwave and add ¼ cup couscous to each cup.

10. Cover the couscous cups with a plate and allow to sit for 5 minutes.

11. Place 3 chicken strips on top of your couscous cups. Then add a mint leaf to each cup and serve.

Carrot Cupcakes

These cupcakes are packed with Vitamin A. Enjoy with the frosting or pop 'em into your mouth plain.

Ingredients for 6 cupcakes:

Cupcakes

1 cup all-purpose flour
1 cup sugar
1 teaspoon baking soda
1 teaspoon cinnamon
1 egg
½ cup vegetable oil
1 teaspoon vanilla
⅛ cup crushed pineapple
¾ cup grated carrots

Frosting

8 tablespoons whipped cream cheese
3 tablespoons butter
1 cup powdered sugar
½ teaspoon vanilla

To Make the Cupcakes

1. Preheat the oven to 350°F.

2. Add all the dry ingredients to a bowl.

3. With adult help, mix together the wet ingredients, pineapple, and the carrots with an electric mixer for 2 minutes, until well blended. ⚠

4. Add the dry ingredients to the wet ingredients and continue to mix. ⚠

5. Spoon the batter into the cups, filling each one two-thirds full.

6. Place the cups on a baking sheet and bake for 20 minutes, or until a toothpick comes out clean. ⚠

7. Allow to cool for 10 minutes before frosting.

To Make the Frosting

1. In a bowl, mix together all the frosting ingredients with a fork until well blended.

2. Place the frosting in the refrigerator and chill for 20 minutes.

3. Remove from the refrigerator and use a butter knife to generously frost your cupcakes.

TRY IT THIS WAY!

Cupcakes are the ultimate parties in a cup! Be creative with frosting—add a dollop, or spread it generously all over the top. Add some grated carrot to the top for a touch of color!

What a Party!

There's nothing like bringing your friends and family together over delicious treats you cooked yourself and then hearing, "That was the best party ever!" Remember: The key to making the party memorable is keeping the details in mind, and adding your own special touch to what you prepare and how you decorate.

Enjoy your silicone cups, and may you have the best party—or parties—ever!

About the Author

Julia Myall has worked as a chef in many premier San Francisco restaurants and as a cooking teacher at the American Embassy in Paris. She is the author of *Cook It in a Cup!* and she has thrown countless parties for her three wonderful children. She lives in Lafayette, California.